ORDER OF CHRISTIAN FUNERALS

VIGIL AND FUNERAL MASS

GEOFFREY
CHAPMAN

CONTENTS

VIGIL FOR THE DECEASED WITH RECEPTION   3

VIGIL WITHOUT RECEPTION   5

FUNERAL MASS   12

FUNERAL MASS WITH RECEPTION   15

VIGIL FOR THE DECEASED WITH RECEPTION

At the vigil the community calls on the Father of mercy to receive the person who has died into the kingdom of light and peace.

This rite is used when the body of the person who has died is brought into the church. If the body has already been received, turn to p. 5.

The minister greets the family and other mourners at the door of the church.

INTRODUCTORY RITES

Greeting

Stand. After the minister's greeting the response is:

All   **And also with you.**

Sprinkling with Holy Water

The minister may sprinkle the coffin with holy water. This sprinkling is a reminder of baptism.

Entrance Procession

This is a symbol of the journey of the deceased. During the procession all join in a psalm or song.

Placing of the Pall and of Christian Symbols

The pall, which symbolizes the baptismal garment, may be placed on the coffin.

A symbol of the Christian life, such as a Book of the Gospels, a Bible, or a cross, may be carried in procession and placed on the coffin.

Invitation to Prayer

The minister invites all who are present to pray for the person who has died. All pray in silence.

Opening Prayer

The minister leads the prayer. At the end all respond:

All   **Amen.**

Turn to p. 6.

VIGIL WITHOUT RECEPTION

At the vigil the community calls on the Father of mercy to receive the person who has died into the kingdom of light and peace.

INTRODUCTORY RITES

Greeting

Stand. The minister greets those present. The response is:

All **And also with you.**

Opening Song

Invitation to Prayer

The minister invites all who are present to pray for the person who has died. All pray in silence.

Opening Prayer

The minister leads the prayer. At the end all respond:

All **Amen.**

LITURGY OF THE WORD

God speaks through the Scripture readings to meet the needs, sorrows, fears and hopes of those present.

FIRST READING

Sit. A text from the Old or New Testament is proclaimed. The Reader concludes with:

Reader	This is the Word of the Lord.
All	**Thanks be to God.**

RESPONSORIAL PSALM

    R.   **The Lord is my light and my help.**

or

    R.   **I am sure I shall see the Lord's goodness in the land of the living.**

Psalm 26 (27)

The Lord is my light and my help;
whom shall I fear?
The Lord is the stronghold of my life;
before whom shall I shrink? R.

There is one thing I ask of the Lord,
for this I long,
to live in the house of the Lord
all the days of my life,
to savour the sweetness of the Lord,
to behold his temple. R.

O Lord, hear my voice when I call;
have mercy and answer.
It is your face, O Lord, that I seek;
hide not your face. R.

I am sure I shall see the Lord's goodness
in the land of the living.
Hope in him, hold firm and take heart.
Hope in the Lord! R.

Response   PAUL INWOOD

The Lord is my light and my help.

For the psalm-tone see p. 32.

Alternative Response   GEOFFREY BOULTON SMITH

I am sure I shall see the Lord's good–ness in the land of the liv–ing.

For the psalm-tone see p. 34.

For a child

R. **The Lord is my shepherd; there is nothing I shall want.**

Psalm 22 (23)

The Lord is my shepherd;
there is nothing I shall want.
Fresh and green are the pastures
where he gives me repose.
Near restful waters he leads me,
to revive my drooping spirit. R.

He guides me along the right path;
he is true to his name.
If I should walk in the valley of darkness
no evil would I fear.
You are there with your crook and your staff;
with these you give me comfort. R.

You have prepared a banquet for me
in the sight of my foes.
My head you have anointed with oil;
my cup is overflowing. R.

Surely goodness and kindness shall follow me
all the days of my life.
In the Lord's own house shall I dwell
for ever and ever. R.

Response   JAMES WALSH

For the psalm-tone see p. 35.

Alternative words on p. 36 to the tune Crimond.

GOSPEL

If a deacon or priest proclaims the gospel he says:

Deacon or priest	The Lord be with you.
All	**And also with you.**
Minister	A reading from the holy gospel according to N.
All	**Glory to you, Lord.**

At the end of the gospel:

Minister	This is the gospel of the Lord.
All	**Praise to you, Lord Jesus Christ.**

HOMILY

The homily helps the community to understand how the Scripture readings reveal God's love and his victory over death.

PRAYER OF INTERCESSION

LITANY

The response is:

All   **Lord, have mercy.**

---

or, if the deceased is a child

All   **Bless us and keep us, O Lord.**

The Lord's Prayer

After the minister's invitation:

> All   Our Father, who art in heaven,
> hallowed be thy name;
> thy kingdom come;
> thy will be done on earth as it is in heaven.
> Give us this day our daily bread;
> and forgive us our trespasses
> as we forgive those who trespass against us;
> and lead us not into temptation,
> but deliver us from evil.

CONCLUDING RITE

Blessing

> Minister   Blessed are those who have died in the Lord;
> let them rest from their labours for their good deeds go with them.

---

or, if the deceased is a child

> Minister   Jesus said: 'Let the children come to me. Do not keep them from me. The Kingdom of God belongs to such as these.'

> Minister   Eternal rest grant unto him/her, O Lord.
> All   **And let perpetual light shine upon him/her.**
>
> Minister   May he/she rest in peace.
> All   **Amen.**
>
> Minister   May his/her soul and the souls of all the faithful departed, through the mercy of God, rest in peace.
> All   **Amen.**

A A minister who is a priest or deacon says:

May the peace of God,
which is beyond all understanding,
keep your hearts and minds
in the knowledge and love of God
and of his Son, our Lord Jesus Christ.
All   **Amen.**

May almighty God bless you,
the Father, and the Son, ✠ and the Holy Spirit.
All   **Amen.**

or

B A minister who is a priest or deacon says:

May the love of God and the peace of the Lord Jesus Christ
console you
and gently wipe every tear from your eyes:
All   **Amen.**

May almighty God bless you,
the Father, and the Son, ✠ and the Holy Spirit.
All   **Amen.**

or

C A lay minister invokes God's blessing and signs himself or herself with the sign of the cross, saying:

May the love of God and the peace of the Lord Jesus Christ
bless and console us
and gently wipe every tear from our eyes:
in the name of the Father,
and of the Son, and of the Holy Spirit.
All   **Amen.**

The vigil may conclude with a song or a few moments of silent prayer or both.

FUNERAL MASS

By the celebration of the Eucharist the members of the community express their faith in Jesus' presence among them, and in union with the whole Church offer prayers and petitions for the deceased, whom they entrust to God's merciful love.

Mass begins here when the body of the person who died has already been brought into the church. If the body is to be received, turn to p. 15.

INTRODUCTORY RITES

ENTRANCE SONG

Priest	**In the name of the Father, and of the Son, and of the Holy Spirit.**
All	**Amen.**

GREETING

The priest greets those present.

All **And also with you.**

PENITENTIAL RITE

The priest invites the people to acknowledge their sinfulness and to ask forgiveness.

After a pause for silent reflection:

A	All	I confess to almighty God, and to you, my brothers and sisters, that I have sinned through my own fault in my thoughts and in my words, in what I have done, and in what I have failed to do; and I ask blessed Mary, ever virgin, all the angels and saints, and you, my brothers and sisters, to pray for me to the Lord our God.
	Priest	May almighty God have mercy on us, forgive us our sins, and bring us to everlasting life.
	All	**Amen.**
	Priest	Lord, have mercy.
	All	**Lord, have mercy.**
	Priest	Christ, have mercy.
	All	**Christ, have mercy.**
	Priest	Lord, have mercy.
	All	**Lord, have mercy.**

or

B	Priest	Lord, we have sinned against you: Lord, have mercy.
	All	**Lord, have mercy.**
	Priest	Lord, show us your mercy and love.
	All	**And grant us your salvation.**
	Priest	May almighty God have mercy on us, forgive us our sins, and bring us to everlasting life.
	All	**Amen.**
	Priest	Lord, have mercy.
	All	**Lord, have mercy.**
	Priest	Christ, have mercy.
	All	**Christ, have mercy.**
	Priest	Lord, have mercy.
	All	**Lord, have mercy.**

or

C   The priest makes the invocation to which the response is:

	Priest	Lord, have mercy.
	All	**Lord, have mercy.**
	Priest	Christ, have mercy.
	All	**Christ, have mercy.**
	Priest	Lord, have mercy.
	All	**Lord, have mercy.**

Priest May almighty God have mercy on us,
        forgive us our sins,
        and bring us to everlasting life.
All   **Amen.**

Opening Prayer

The priest invites the assembly to pray, and a short time is spent in silent prayer. After the prayer all respond:

All   **Amen.**

Turn to p. 16.

FUNERAL MASS WITH RECEPTION

INTRODUCTORY RITES

Greeting

The priest greets the people.

All   **And also with you.**

Sprinkling with Holy Water

The priest may sprinkle the coffin with holy water. This is a reminder that through baptism the deceased was marked for eternal life.

Entrance Procession and Song

The Easter candle may be placed beforehand near the position the coffin will occupy at the conclusion of the procession.

Placing of the Pall and of Christian Symbols

The pall, which symbolizes the baptismal garment, may be placed on the coffin.

A symbol of the Christian life, such as a Book of the Gospels, a Bible or a cross, may be carried in procession and placed on the coffin.

Opening Prayer

Priest   Let us pray.

A pause for silent prayer follows. After the prayer all respond:

All   **Amen.**

LITURGY OF THE WORD

God speaks through the Scripture readings to meet the needs, sorrows, fears and hopes of those present.

First Reading

Sit. A text from the Old or New Testament is proclaimed. The Reader concludes with:

Reader	**This is the Word of the Lord.**
All	**Thanks be to God.**

Responsorial Psalm

A second reading from the New Testament may follow.

Gospel

All stand to greet the gospel. A gospel acclamation such as one of the following is sung.

JACQUES BERTHIER

Al - le - lu - ia, al - le - lu - ia, al - le - lu —— ia! Al - le -
lu - ia, al - le - lu - ia, al - le - lu —— ia!

or

Response

GERRY FITZPATRICK

Al — le - lu — ia, al - le - lu - ia,
Al — le - lu — ia, al - le - lu - ia.

For accompaniment see p. 37.

If a deacon or priest proclaims the gospel he says:

Deacon or priest	The Lord be with you.
All	**And also with you.**
Deacon or priest	A reading from the holy gospel according to N.
All	**Glory to you, Lord.**

At the end of the gospel:

Deacon or priest	This is the gospel of the Lord.
All	**Praise to you, Lord Jesus Christ.**

Homily

> The homily helps the community to understand how the Scripture readings reveal God's love and his victory over death.

General Intercessions

> In the intercessions we respond to the Word of God by prayer for the deceased person, all who have died, those who mourn and all members of the community.

Each petition concludes:

Reader	Lord, in your mercy:
All	**Hear our prayer.**

or

Reader	We pray to the Lord:
All	**Lord, hear our prayer.**

or

Reader	Lord, hear us:
All	**Lord, graciously hear us:**

For a child

Reader	Let us pray to the Lord:
All	**Lord, have mercy.**

or

Reader	To you we pray:
All	**Bless us and keep us, O Lord.**

LITURGY OF THE EUCHARIST

In the Liturgy of the Eucharist, we repeat the words and actions of Christ at the Last Supper when he took the bread and wine, gave thanks and said, This is my body, this is my blood. Do this in memory of me'. When we share in this sacrifice we share in the victory over death Christ won for us through death and resurrection.

PREPARATION OF THE GIFTS

The bread and wine for the eucharist are brought to the altar. If there is no music the priest may say the following prayers aloud:

Priest	Blessed are you, Lord, God of all creation. Through your goodness we have this bread to offer, which earth has given and human hands have made. It will become for us the bread of life.
All	**Blessed be God for ever.**
Priest	Blessed are you, Lord, God of all creation. Through your goodness we have this wine to offer, fruit of the vine and work of human hands. It will become our spiritual drink.
All	**Blessed be God for ever.**

The priest then invites those present to pray:

All stand.

Priest	Pray, brethren, that our sacrifice may be acceptable to God, the almighty Father.
All	**May the Lord accept the sacrifice at your hands for the praise and glory of his name, for our good, and the good of all his Church.**
Priest	Let us pray...
All	**Amen.**

EUCHARISTIC PRAYER

Priest	The Lord be with you.
All	**And also with you.**
Priest	Lift up your hearts.
All	**We lift them up to the Lord.**
Priest	Let us give thanks to the Lord our God.
All	**It is right to give him thanks and praise.**

At the end of the Preface all sing or say:

All Holy, holy, holy Lord, God of power and might,
heaven and earth are full of your glory.
Hosanna in the highest.
Blessed is he who comes in the name of the Lord.
Hosanna in the highest.

PAUL INWOOD

The priest continues the Eucharistic Prayer. After the narrative of the Lord's Supper he sings or says:

Priest   Let us proclaim the mystery of faith.

Those present sing or say one of the following:

A   Christ has died,
Christ is risen,
Christ will come again.

or

B   Dying you destroyed our death,
rising you restored our life.
Lord Jesus, come in glory.

or

C   When we eat this bread and drink this cup,
we proclaim your death, Lord Jesus,
until you come in glory.

or

D   Lord, by your cross and resurrection
you have set us free.
You are the Saviour of the world.

A

GERRY FITZPATRICK

Priest: Let us proclaim the myst-'ry of faith:

All: Christ has died. Christ is ri-sen. Christ will come a-gain.

The Eucharistic Prayer continues and concludes with the following doxology which is sung or said by the priest:

Priest   Through him,
         with him,
         in him,
         in the unity of the Holy Spirit,
         all glory and honour is yours,
         almighty Father,
         for ever and ever.
All   Amen.

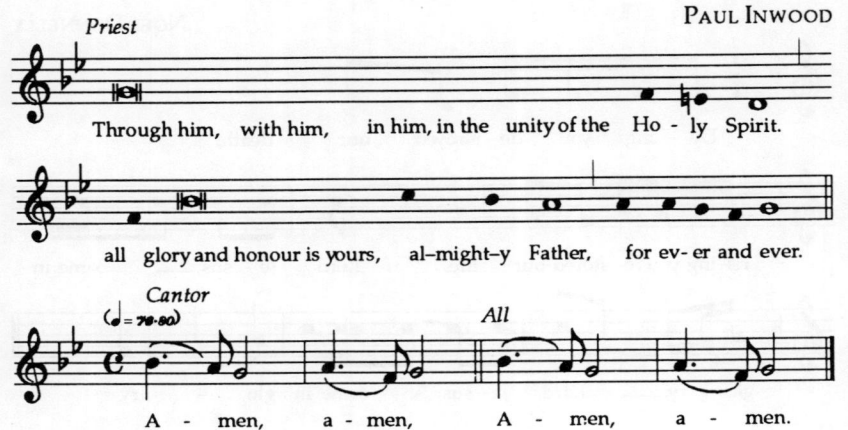

COMMUNION RITE

The Lord's Prayer

The priest invites those present to pray the Lord's Prayer.

All stand.

All	**Our Father, who art in heaven,** **hallowed be thy name;** **thy kingdom come;** **thy will be done on earth as it is in heaven.** **Give us this day our daily bread;** **and forgive us our trespasses** **as we forgive those who trespass against us;** **and lead us not into temptation,** **but deliver us from evil.**
Priest	Deliver us, Lord, from every evil, and grant us peace in our day. In your mercy keep us free from sin and protect us from all anxiety as we wait in joyful hope for the coming of our Saviour, Jesus Christ.
All	**For the kingdom, the power, and the glory are yours,** **now and for ever.**
Priest	Lord Jesus Christ, you said to your apostles: I leave you peace, my peace I give you. Look not on our sins, but on the faith of your Church, and grant us the peace and unity of your kingdom where you live for ever and ever.
All	**Amen.**
Priest	The peace of the Lord be with you always.
All	**And also with you.**

Deacon or priest Let us offer each other the sign of peace.

All greet each other with a sign of peace.

Lamb of God

All Lamb of God, you take away the sins of the world: have mercy on us.
Lamb of God, you take away the sins of the world: have mercy on us.
Lamb of God, you take away the sins of the world: grant us peace.

STEPHEN DEAN

Communion

Priest   This is the Lamb of God
who takes away the sins of the world.
Happy are those who are called to his supper.

All   **Lord, I am not worthy to receive you,
but only say the word and I shall be healed.**

Communion may be received from the chalice as well as under the form of bread.

During the communion procession a song may be sung. After communion a period of silence or a song may follow.

Prayer after Communion

Priest   Let us pray...
All   **Amen.**

If the final commendation is to be celebrated at the place of committal, the procession to the place of committal now takes place (see p. 29).

FINAL COMMENDATION

Following the prayer after communion, the priest goes to a place near the coffin.

A member of the family or a friend of the deceased may speak in remembrance of the deceased before the final commendation begins.

Invitation to Prayer

The priest now invites those present to pray; silent prayer follows.

Signs of Farewell

The coffin may now be incensed and sprinkled with holy water.

Song of Farewell

One of the following or another suitable hymn or song may be sung.

A I know that my Redeemer lives,
And on that final day of days,
His voice shall bid me rise again:
Unending joy, unceasing praise!

This hope I cherish in my heart:
To stand on earth, my flesh restored,
And not a stranger but a friend,
Behold my Saviour and my Lord.

Tune: LM, for example, Wareham

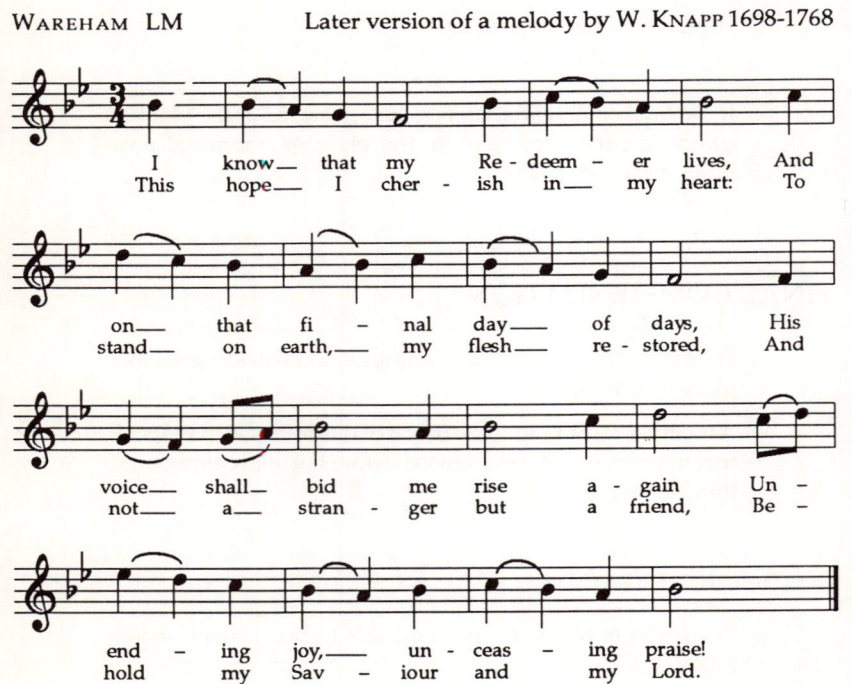

Wareham LM — Later version of a melody by W. Knapp 1698-1768

Or the alternative on p. 44.

or

B Saints of God, come to his/her aid!
Hasten to meet him/her, angels of the Lord!
R. **Receive his/her soul and present him/her
to God the Most High.**

Eternal rest grant unto him/her, O Lord,
and let perpetual light shine upon him/her.
R. **Receive his/her soul and present him/her
to God the Most High.**

COELITES PLAUDANT   ROUEN ANTIPHONER, 1728

or   **GERRY FITZPATRICK**

This is part of 'Receive his Soul' printed in full with accompaniment on pp. 46-47.

Prayer of Commendation

> Priest   ... We ask this through Christ our Lord.
> All   **Amen.**

PROCESSION TO THE PLACE OF COMMITTAL

At the conclusion of the funeral liturgy, the procession is formed and the body is accompanied to the place of committal.

Deacon or priest   In peace let us take N. to his/her place of rest.

If a symbol of the Christian life has been placed on the coffin, it is removed at this time.

The procession then begins: the priest and assisting ministers precede the coffin; the family and mourners follow.

A hymn or song may be sung during the procession to the entrance of the church. The singing may continue during the journey to the place of committal.

A   The following antiphon may be sung with verses from Psalm 24 (25).

> May the angels lead you into paradise;
> may the martyrs come to welcome you
> and take you to the holy city,
> the new and eternal Jerusalem.

or

B   The following antiphon may be sung with verses from Psalms 114-115 (116) or separately.

> May choirs of angels welcome you
> and lead you to the bosom of Abraham;
> and where Lazarus is poor no longer
> may you find eternal rest.

or

C May saints and angels lead you on,
Escorting you where Christ has gone.
Now he has called you, come to him
Who sits above the seraphim.

Come to the peace of Abraham
And to the supper of the Lamb:
Come to the glory of the blessed,
And to perpetual light and rest.

Tune: LM, for example Wareham

WAREHAM LM   Later version of a melody by W. KNAPP 1698-1768

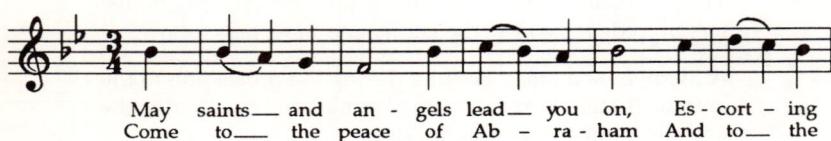

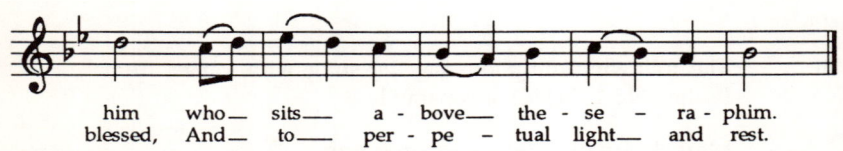

Alternative words to A and B combined which fit a 10 10 10 10 10 10 tune such as Unde et Memores:

May flights of angels lead you on your way
To paradise, and heaven's eternal day!
May martyrs greet you after death's dark night,
And bid you enter into Sion's light!
May choirs of angels sing you to your rest
With one poor Laz'rus, now for ever blest!

Text: In paradisum, tr. James Quinn, SJ

Unde et Memores 10 10. 10 10. 10 10   William Henry Monk 1823-89

PSALM 26 (27)

Paul Inwood

Response: The Lord is my light and my help.

Psalm-Tone [6-line verse only]

1. The Lord is my light and | my | help;
   whom shall | I | fear?
   The Lord is the stronghold | of my | life;
   before whom shall | I | shrink? R.

2. There is one thing I ask of | the | Lord,
   for this | I | long,
   to live in the house of | the | Lord
   all the days of | my | life,
   to savour the sweetness | of the | Lord,
   to behold | his | temple. R.

3. O Lord, hear my voice when | I | call;
   have mercy | and | answer.
   It is your face, O Lord, that | I | seek;
   hide not | your | face. R.

4. I am sure I shall see the | Lord's | goodness
   in the land of | the | living.
   Hope in him, hold firm | and take | heart.
   Hope in | the | Lord. R.

Alternative Response — GEOFFREY BOULTON SMITH

1. The Lórd is my líght and my hélp;
   whóm shall I féar?
   The Lórd is • the strónghold • of my lífe;
   before whóm shall I • shrínk? R.

2. There is óne thing I ásk of the Lórd,
   for thís I lóng,
   to líve in • the hóuse of the Lórd
   all the dáys of • my lífe,
   to sávour •the swéetness •of the Lórd,
   to behóld his témple. R.

3. O Lórd, hear my vóice when I cáll;
   have mércy and ánswer.
   Of yóu my héart has spóken:
   'Séek his fáce.' R.

4. I am súre I shall sée the Lord's góodness
   in the lánd of the líving.
   Hope in hím, hold fírm and take héart.
   Hópe in • the Lórd. R.

Psalm-Tone JOSEPH GELINEAU, adapted G.B.S.

WAREHAM LM Later version of a melody by W. KNAPP 1698-1768

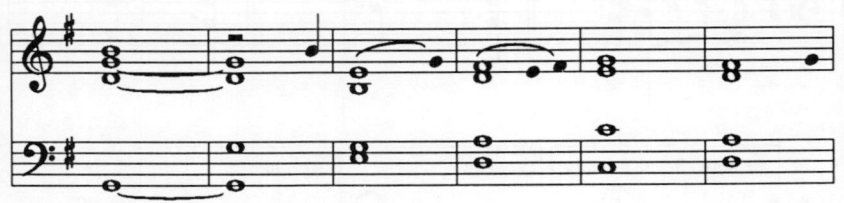

PSALM 22 (23)

Response — JAMES WALSH

Gently flowing

The Lord is my shepherd; there is nothing I shall want.

Psalm-Tone

1. The Lord | is my | shepherd;
   there is nothing | I shall want.
   Fresh and | green are the | pastures
   where he | gives me re | pose. R

2. Near restful wa | ters he | leads me,
   to revive my | drooping | spirit.
   He guides me along the right | path;
   he is | true to his | name. R

3. If I should walk in the vall | ey of | darkness
   no evil | would I | fear.
   You are there with your | crook and your | staff;
   with these you | give me com | fort. R

4. You have prepared a ban | quet for | me
   in the sight | of my | foes.
   My head you have a | nointed with | oil;
   my cup | is over | flowing. R

5. Surely goodness and kind | ness shall | follow me
   all the days | of my | life.
   In the Lord's own | house shall I | dwell
   for | ever and | ever. R.

CRIMOND CM   JESSIE IRVINE 1836-87

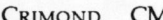

1. The Lord's my shepherd, I'll not want,
   He makes me down to lie
   In pastures green; he leadeth me
   The quiet waters by.

2. My soul he doth restore again,
   And me to walk doth make
   Within the paths of righteousness,
   E'en for his own name's sake.

3. Yea, though I walk through death's dark vale,
   Yet will I fear no ill;
   For thou art with me, and thy rod
   And staff me comfort still.

4. My table thou hast furnished
   In presence of my foes;
   My head thou dost with oil anoint,
   And my cup overflows.

5. Goodness and mercy all my life
   Shall surely follow me;
   And in God's house for evermore
   My dwelling-place shall be.

W. Whittingham, F. Rous and others
From the *Scottish Psalter* 1650

ALTERNATIVE GOSPEL ACCLAMATION
IF WE HAVE DIED

GERRY FITZPATRICK

HOLY, HOLY

Paul Inwood

DOXOLOGY and AMEN

Paul Inwood

LAMB OF GOD

Stephen Dean

I KNOW THAT MY REDEEMER LIVES

GERRY FITZPATRICK

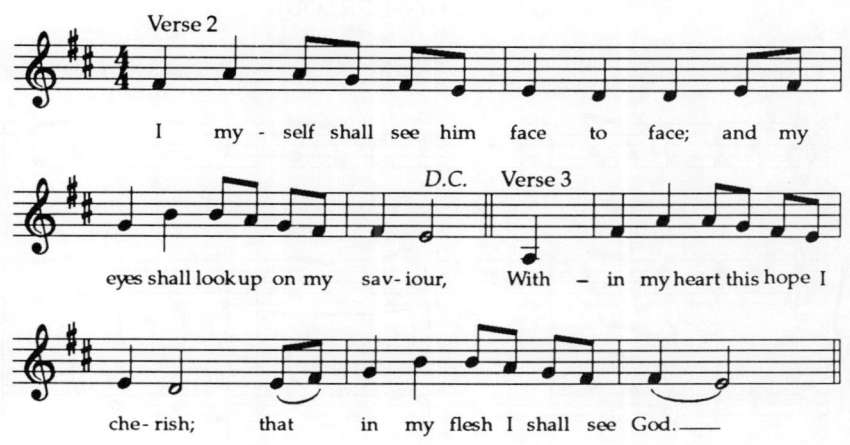

COELITES PLAUDANT   ROUEN ANTIPHONER, 1728

RECEIVE HIS/HER SOUL

GERRY FITZPATRICK

UNDE ET MEMORES 10 10. 10 10. 10 10   WILLIAM HENRY MONK 1823-89